Scary Creatures
BIG CATS

Written by
Penny Clarke

Illustrated by
Terry Riley

Created and designed by
David Salariya

BOOK HOUSE

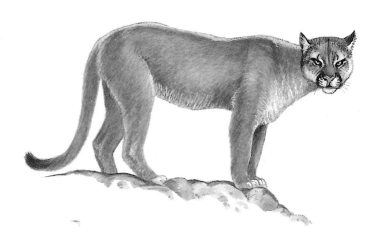

Author:

Penny Clarke is an author and editor specialising in information books for children. The books she has written include titles on natural history, rainforests and volcanoes, as well as others on different periods of history. She used to live in central London, but thanks to modern technology she has now realised her dream of being able to live and work in the countryside.

Artist:

Terry Riley worked for many years as an art director in advertising before writing and illustrating his own series of children's books. He is passionate about natural history and has illustrated hundreds of wildlife projects for publishing, film and television.

Additional artists:
Mark Bergin
Robert Morton
Carolyn Scrace
David Stewart

Series creator:

David Salariya was born in Dundee, Scotland. In 1989 he established The Salariya Book Company. He has illustrated a wide range of books and has created many new series for publishers in the UK and overseas. He lives in Brighton with his wife, illustrator Shirley Willis, and their son.

Consultant:

Dr Gerald Legg holds a doctorate in zoology from Manchester University. He worked in West Africa for several years as a lecturer and rainforest researcher and his current position is biologist at the Booth Museum of Natural History in Brighton. He is also the author of many natural history books for children.

Editor: Karen Barker Smith

Picture research: Nicky Roe

Photographic credits:

Corbis Images: 18, 19
John Foxx Images: 5, 13, 15, 16, 17, 21
T Kitchin & V Hurst, NHPA: 10
PhotoDisc: 11
Christophe Ratier, NHPA: 12
RSPCA: 29
Kevin Schafer, NHPA: 22

Published in Great Britain in 2003 by
Book House, an imprint of
The Salariya Book Company Ltd
25 Marlborough Place, Brighton BN1 1UB

Visit the Salariya Book Company at
www.salariya.com
www.book-house.co.uk

A catalogue record for this book is available from the British Library.

ISBN 1 904194 40 0

Printed in China.

Printed on paper from sustainable forests.

Contents

What is a big cat?

There are about 35 species of wild cat. They are all carnivores and hunt and catch their food. The six largest species are known as the 'big cats'. These are the lion, tiger, jaguar, leopard, cheetah and snow leopard. But some experts disagree with this. They argue that the true big cats are only those that roar. If they are right, only the lion, tiger, leopard and jaguar are truly big cats.

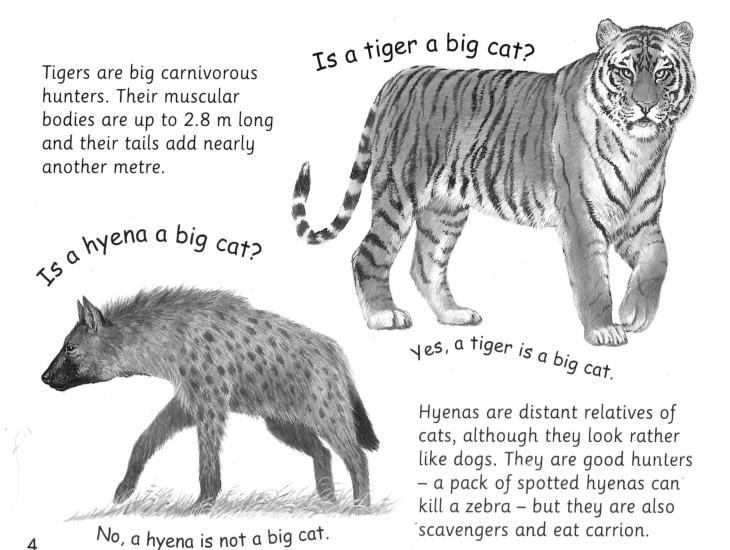

Tigers are big carnivorous hunters. Their muscular bodies are up to 2.8 m long and their tails add nearly another metre.

Is a tiger a big cat?

Is a hyena a big cat?

Yes, a tiger is a big cat.

No, a hyena is not a big cat.

Hyenas are distant relatives of cats, although they look rather like dogs. They are good hunters – a pack of spotted hyenas can kill a zebra – but they are also scavengers and eat carrion.

A panther – a type of leopard

Why are big cats scary?

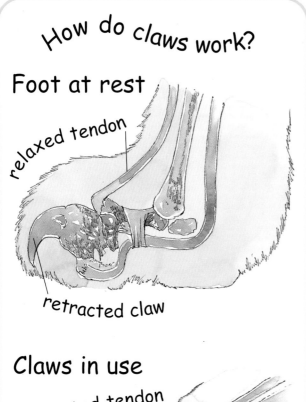

How do claws work?

Foot at rest

relaxed tendon

retracted claw

Claws in use

contracted tendon

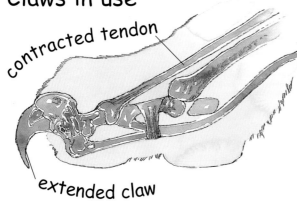

extended claw

All cats have long, sharp, retractile claws. They use them to grasp prey and grip tree trunks when they climb. When cats are not grasping or climbing they retract their claws within their footpads. The cheetah is the only cat that cannot do this.

An adult lion's body is about 2 m long even without the tail. Perhaps it is this large size that makes such big cats scary. Most big cats can roar very loudly and this can be frightening. We know that big cats are faster and stronger than humans. Apart from a gun, we have no defence against a hungry big cat.

X-Ray Vision

Hold the page opposite up to the light and see what's inside a lion.

See what's inside

hairy mane

large paws

long tail for balance

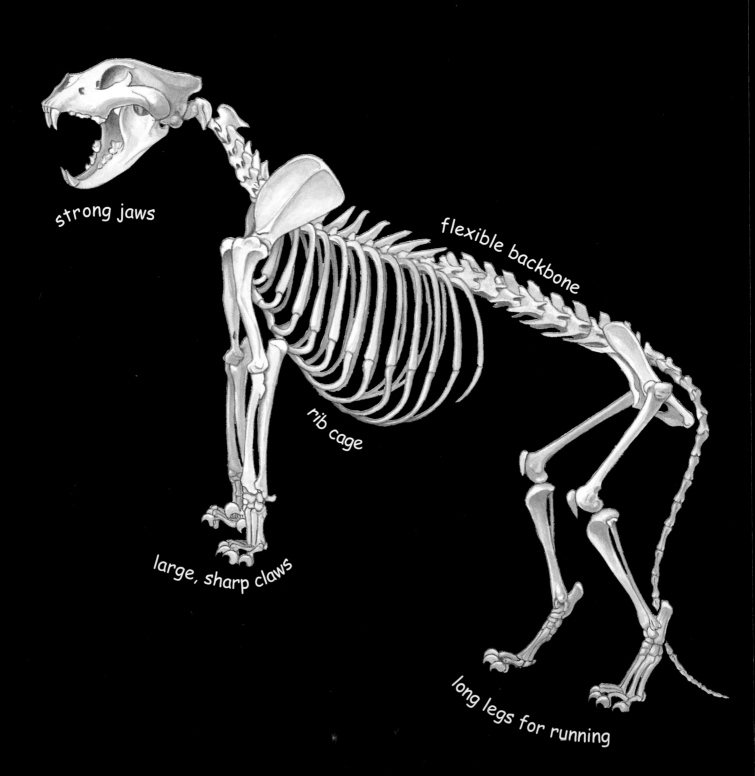

What's inside a big cat?

All cats, whatever their size, have bodies perfect for hunting. They have broad rib cages so there is plenty of room for their lungs. They need to breathe fast when they are running at speed. Their flexible backbones help them twist and turn as they chase after their prey.

Big cats have powerful jaws so they can kill with a single bite to the neck. If they don't kill instantly their prey might escape.

Human

Leopard

Leopards are smaller than lions and tigers, but are still larger and more powerful than any human. Like most big cats, the males and females are the same size: about 1.9 m long with tails of nearly 1.4 m.

canine teeth

carnassial teeth

Cats are hunters. They kill with a bite of their long dagger-like canine teeth. When they eat, they tear through flesh with their carnassial teeth (right).

Skull of a leopard

9

What do big cats eat?

Big cats are carnivores – they eat other living creatures. The bigger the big cat, the bigger its prey. Lions will hunt buffalo and giraffes, which are much bigger than they are. Tigers hunt gaurs, which are large wild relatives of cows. If their normal prey is hard to find, big cats will eat small animals like mice and hares. Leopards will even scavenge meat they have not caught themselves.

Did you know?

The mountain lion lives on the American continent, from Canada in the north to the mountains of South America. It is also called the puma, silver lion and cougar. Its food ranges from large mule deer to small snowshoe hares.

10 Mountain lion with its prey – a snowshoe hare

Male lion killing a zebra

Lions live in groups. After they have killed, members of the group gather to eat the prey. The cubs are not allowed to eat before the adults. Leopards live alone and when they kill large prey they drag it up a tree so they can eat it without hyenas or vultures trying to grab it.

wildebeest

antelope

baboon

hare

boar

zebra

deer   dog

Big cat prey

Do all big cats hunt?

Snow leopards live in the Himalayas and the mountains of Russia and northern Asia. They hunt mountain animals like ibex and boar, as well as ground-nesting birds.

Lions and leopards hunt antelope and zebras, and leopards also hunt baboons. In winter, the snowshoe hares hunted by mountain lions turn white, to match the snow covering the ground. This makes hunting them more difficult.

Jaguars, which live mostly in Central and South America, hunt tapirs, deer, otters and even turtles and caiman.

Yes, all big cats hunt.

Are big cats good hunters?

Big cats are the best hunters in the world. Their flexible, muscular bodies, excellent eyesight and speed make it difficult for their prey to escape. Lions and jaguars are not as fast as the other big cats, but make up for this in other ways. Lions often hunt in a group and jaguars are superb stalkers.

Did you know?

Cheetahs are the fastest of the big cats. They watch their prey from long grass, then slowly stalk it before leaping out and running it down. As cheetahs run, at speeds of up to 112 kph, their long tail helps them keep their balance.

12 Cheetah chasing a gazelle

Leopard preparing to pounce on its prey

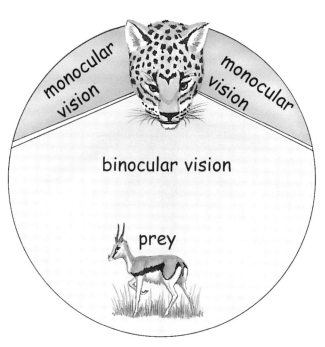

Big cat eyesight

Big cats' large, forward-looking eyes give them binocular vision (left), just like humans. This means they can judge distances accurately, which is essential for successful hunting.

Most big cats stalk their prey, although leopards will often drop on their victims from a tree (above). A stalk begins with the big cat downwind of its prey. That means the cat's scent is blown away from the animal it is hunting. If the hunted animal smelt the cat it would be off in a flash. The cat creeps forward, often on its stomach. Then, when it is very close, it pounces or gives chase.

When a cheetah runs it stretches its spine as it leaps through the air and bounds along.

How fast can big cats run?

A cheetah can run extremely fast, reaching a speed of 112 kph. When it gets to its prey it knocks it sideways, then kills it by biting its throat. But a cheetah is a sprinter, not a long-distance runner. If it does not catch its prey quickly it gives up the chase. If the cheetah continued it would just be a waste of energy because the prey would escape as the cheetah slowed down.

Can cheetahs run faster than lions?

The cheetah is fast because it has a slender, streamlined body. Compare the pictures on this page with those of the tiger on page 4 and the lion on page 7. The cheetah's long legs and a flexible spine also help.

Yes, cheetahs are the fastest big cats.

 ## Did you know?

Cheetahs cannot run at top speed for more than about 550 m. Sometimes a cheetah family group works together, taking it in turns to chase and exhaust animals such as zebras which can run fast for great distances.

Do cheetahs stalk their prey?

Cheetahs live in the open grasslands of Africa called savannahs. In the savannah there are few trees and bushes for cheetahs to hide in while hunting. Instead they have to crouch and stalk through the long grass before making a final dash across open ground to their prey.

Yes, cheetahs stalk their prey.

Cheetah walking on the savannah

Why do leopards have spots?

Leopards have spots for camouflage. Camouflage is a type of disguise – it makes something difficult to see. The spots and patterns on big cats' coats break up their outline, helping them to blend in with their surroundings (below). This makes them even more difficult for their prey to see.

Why do tigers have stripes?

Tigers live in forests and woodland. Sunlight shining through the trees makes shadows on the ground. The tiger's dark stripes look like shadows. They break up the outline of its body, helping to camouflage it as it stalks its prey among the trees.

Tigers' stripes are for camouflage.

Cheetah camouflaged in long grass

Male lion

Did you know?

Lions' coats range in colour from a pale yellow-brown to a rich reddish-brown. These colours help them blend in with the dry grasslands of southern Africa where they live. Only male lions have manes (above). The mane helps make the lion look even larger and fiercer.

Are big cats good parents?

Female big cats are excellent mothers. They will attack anything that threatens their cubs. Most big cats are solitary, so the cubs are reared just by their mother. In fact, the female will attack and drive away the cubs' father if he comes near them.

Did you know?

Lions are the only big cats to live in groups. Each group, or pride, is usually made up of about three adult males, 15 females and their cubs. When the male cubs are about 18 months old they are driven away to find a territory and a mate for themselves.

Lioness with her cubs

Young cheetahs with their mother

Do cubs stay with their mother?

Most big cat cubs will stay with their mother until they are between 18 months and two years old.

Tiger cubs are with their mothers for several years. Like all mammals, tiger cubs feed on their mothers' milk for the first few months. Then she starts bringing them food she has caught. By the time they are six months old the cubs begin hunting with their mother. Gradually they learn the skills they will need to survive when they leave her care.

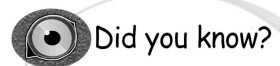 Did you know?

Leopards often give birth to their cubs in a hole in a tree, where they will be safe when their mother goes out hunting.

Yes, most big cat cubs stay with their mother until they are fully grown.

Do big cats live in cold places?

We think of lions and cheetahs hunting zebras and antelope in the hot grasslands of southern Africa, where leopards sun themselves on tree branches. But the snow leopard lives high in the Himalayas. In summer it hunts birds, mountain sheep and goats among the glaciers and snowfields. In winter it follows its prey down to the lower slopes, about 2,000 m above sea level.

 Did you know?

Snow leopard cubs start hunting with their mothers at two months old – younger than other big cat cubs. Food is difficult to find where they live, so each snow leopard has to cover long distances, too far for the mother to return to her cubs each time.

The snow leopard has thick, beautiful fur to keep it warm. Sadly, it is now rare because it has been hunted for its fur.

Snow leopard

Tiger wading into a river to keep cool

Do tigers like lying in the sun?

Most big cats love lying in the sun. Tigers do not. Millions of years ago tigers lived in areas of Asia with long cold winters. Today, most wild tigers live in the forests of India where the summers are hot. To keep cool they lie in water, especially at midday when it is hottest. If there is no water nearby, they lie in the deepest shade they can find.

No, tigers prefer to lie in the shade.

Tigers used to live throughout much of Asia, from Siberia in the north to Bali in the south. Each region had its own variety of tiger, called a subspecies. The biggest difference between each subspecies was the colour and thickness of its coat. Many of these subspecies are now extinct.

Do big cats have small relatives?

Most species of cat are less than a metre long. They are much smaller than the big cats, but they look very similar. They all have strong muscular bodies. Their heads are short and broad, their eyes are large and they have lots of whiskers around their nose and mouth. Most of them also have long tails.

X-Ray Vision

Hold the page opposite up to the light and see what's inside a domestic cat.

See what's inside

Unlike most cats bobcats have short tails – less than 20 cm long. Bobcats live in forests, woods, swamps and grasslands in western North America and Mexico. They stalk their prey slowly before pouncing and killing it with a bite – just like domestic cats.

22 North American bobcat in winter

Domestic cats are as good at hunting as their wild relations. They kill vermin such as mice and rats, but also kill millions of garden birds each year.

long tail

flexible backbone

skull

This is the skeleton of a domestic cat. Look at the lion's skeleton on page 8 and see how alike they are. If the cat pounces on the mouse its tail will help it keep its balance.

ribs

claws

What do other cats look like?

Wild cats need good camouflage for hunting, so the colour of their fur varies according to where they live. For example, when the pampas cats of South America live in forests their coats are darker than when they live in sunny open grasslands.

Servals (below) live in the woods and plains of southern Africa. Their fur varies enormously. Servals with light brown coats usually have rows of large black spots. Those with darker coats have small spots dotted all over their body.

Did you know?

A few leopards have no camouflage. They have completely black coats and are called panthers (see page 5).

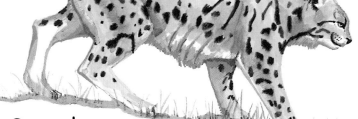

Serval

The caracal (right) is easy to identify. Its long ears with tufts of dark hair at the tips are quite different from those of any other cat.

Caracal

Where do big cats live?

Different species of cat live all over the world and in all types of climate. The true big cats, however, now live only in South America, Asia and Africa.

Big cats need big prey and the animals they hunt now only live in parts of the world with plenty of space and not too many humans.

Mountain lion

No big cats live in North America. The mountain lion, or cougar, is the largest wild cat there.

Jaguars lived in North America until the early 20th century. They are now an endangered species and can only be found in parts of South America.

Jaguar

Lion

Snow leopard

Tiger

Leopard

Cheetah

27

What are big cats afraid of?

Big cats have no natural enemies, they are too big and powerful for other animals to hunt. Before the invention of guns they were safe from humans. Guns changed that, as did the world's ever-increasing human population. As forests are cut down to provide timber and land for farming, there is less space for the big cats and their prey.

No one knows how many tigers there are, but there are probably fewer than 1,000 left in the wild.

Did you know?

These animals (below) have been killed just for their skins, for use as rugs or for coats. It takes the skins of several big cats to make a fur coat, bringing some big cats closer to extinction.

Animal skins confiscated by customs officers

Big cat facts

Tigers are nocturnal, which means they hunt at night. Their eyes are adapted to take in as much light as possible so they can see their prey in the dark. A domestic cat's eyes work in the same way.

The heaviest known Indian tiger weighed 389 kg.

The lynx, a relative of the big cats, lives in the mountains of Spain and Portugal as well in colder northern lands. Its tufted ears and cheeks and very short tail make it easy to recognise.

The heaviest known lion weighed 313 kg when it died.

The cheetah is the fastest land mammal over short distances – 112 kph for 550 m. The fastest land mammal over long distances is the pronghorn antelope – 67 kph for 1.6 km, but a cheetah could never catch a pronghorn. Why? Pronghorns live in North America and cheetahs in southern Africa!

The lion is often called the king of the beasts and kings have often used lions on their flags and coats-of-arms to symbolise their own power and strength.

Many tigers are killed each year so parts of their bodies can be used to make traditional medicines in the Far East. There is no scientific evidence that these 'medicines' work.

Lions were hunted in Europe and north Africa by the Romans. Gladiators fighting with lions in the Colosseum in ancient Rome was a very popular entertainment.

Snow leopards are probably the best jumpers of the big cats. In the mountains where they live there are many deep ravines and leaping them is the best way to get across.

Glossary

adapted Something that is suitable for a particular purpose.

binocular vision The ability to see the same area with both eyes at the same time.

caiman A South American relative of crocodiles and alligators.

camouflage Coloring which helps an animal blend in with its surroundings.

carnivore Any animal that eats the flesh of other animals as its main food source.

carrion Decaying flesh.

extinct Species of animals that are no longer alive anywhere in the world.

mammal An animal that feeds on its mother's milk when it is a baby.

monocular vision The ability of each eye to see a different area at the same time.

nocturnal An animal that is active at night.

predator Any animal that hunts other living creatures for food.

prey Any animal that is hunted by other animals for food.

retractile Claws which can be extended or withdrawn (retracted) into sheaths, like the claws of cats.

scavenger An animal that eats carrion.

solitary An animal that prefers to live alone.

species A group of living things that look alike, behave in the same way, and can interbreed.

subspecies A group of animals in a species that is slightly different from the rest of the species. This is usually because the animals of the subspecies have been isolated from the rest of the species for a long time. For example, the tigers in Siberia are obviously tigers, but look different to those that live in India.

Index